Flight Details

Today's date is...

I am flying from..

I am flying to..

The length of the flight is..............................

My flight number is......................................

The airline is..

The aircraft type is.......................................

My seat number is..

The distance I am flying is............................

Pilot's Comments

....

....

....

....

....

....

....

....

Flight Details

Today's date is..
I am flying from...
I am flying to...
The length of the flight is................................
My flight number is..
The airline is...
The aircraft type is.......................................
My seat number is..
The distance I am flying is................................

Pilot's Comments

....
....
....
....
....
....
....
....

Flight Details

Today's date is...

I am flying from...

I am flying to...

The length of the flight is...

My flight number is...

The airline is...

The aircraft type is...

My seat number is...

The distance I am flying is...

Pilot's Comments

....

....

....

....

....

....

....

....

Flight Details

Today's date is..

I am flying from..

I am flying to..

The length of the flight is..

My flight number is..

The airline is...

The aircraft type is..

My seat number is..

The distance I am flying is..

Pilot's Comments

....

....

....

....

....

....

....

....

Flight Details

Today's date is..

I am flying from..

I am flying to..

The length of the flight is..

My flight number is..

The airline is..

The aircraft type is..

My seat number is..

The distance I am flying is..

Pilot's Comments

....

....

....

....

....

....

....

....

Flight Details

Today's date is...

I am flying from..

I am flying to..

The length of the flight is...

My flight number is..

The airline is...

The aircraft type is...

My seat number is...

The distance I am flying is...

Pilot's Comments

....

....

....

....

....

....

....

....

Flight Details

Today's date is..

I am flying from...

I am flying to...

The length of the flight is...................................

My flight number is...

The airline is..

The aircraft type is...

My seat number is..

The distance I am flying is..................................

Pilot's Comments

....

....

....

....

....

....

....

....

Flight Details

Today's date is..

I am flying from...

I am flying to..

The length of the flight is.................................

My flight number is...

The airline is...

The aircraft type is..

My seat number is..

The distance I am flying is................................

Pilot's Comments

....

....

....

....

....

....

....

....

Flight Details

Today's date is..

I am flying from...

I am flying to...

The length of the flight is..

My flight number is..

The airline is...

The aircraft type is...

My seat number is..

The distance I am flying is..

Pilot's Comments

....

....

....

....

....

....

....

....

Flight Details

Today's date is..

I am flying from...

I am flying to..

The length of the flight is...........................

My flight number is.....................................

The airline is...

The aircraft type is.....................................

My seat number is..

The distance I am flying is.........................

Pilot's Comments

....

....

....

....

....

....

....

....

Flight Details

Today's date is..

I am flying from..

I am flying to..

The length of the flight is..

My flight number is..

The airline is..

The aircraft type is..

My seat number is..

The distance I am flying is..

Pilot's Comments

....

....

....

....

....

....

....

....

Flight Details

Today's date is...

I am flying from...

I am flying to...

The length of the flight is...

My flight number is...

The airline is...

The aircraft type is...

My seat number is...

The distance I am flying is...

Pilot's Comments

....

....

....

....

....

....

....

....

Flight Details

Today's date is...

I am flying from...

I am flying to...

The length of the flight is................................

My flight number is..

The airline is...

The aircraft type is.......................................

My seat number is..

The distance I am flying is................................

Pilot's Comments

....

....

....

....

....

....

....

....

Flight Details

Today's date is...
I am flying from...
I am flying to...
The length of the flight is..
My flight number is..
The airline is...
The aircraft type is..
My seat number is..
The distance I am flying is...

Pilot's Comments

....
....
....
....
....
....
....
....

Flight Details

Today's date is...

I am flying from..

I am flying to...

The length of the flight is...

My flight number is..

The airline is..

The aircraft type is..

My seat number is..

The distance I am flying is..

Pilot's Comments

....

....

....

....

....

....

....

....

Flight Details

Today's date is...

I am flying from...

I am flying to...

The length of the flight is...

My flight number is...

The airline is...

The aircraft type is...

My seat number is...

The distance I am flying is...

Pilot's Comments

....

....

....

....

....

....

....

....

Flight Details

Today's date is...

I am flying from...

I am flying to...

The length of the flight is...

My flight number is...

The airline is...

The aircraft type is...

My seat number is...

The distance I am flying is...

Pilot's Comments

....

....

....

....

....

....

....

....

Flight Details

Today's date is...
I am flying from...
I am flying to...
The length of the flight is...
My flight number is...
The airline is...
The aircraft type is...
My seat number is...
The distance I am flying is...

Pilot's Comments

....
....
....
....
....
....
....
....

Flight Details

Today's date is...

I am flying from...

I am flying to...

The length of the flight is...

My flight number is...

The airline is...

The aircraft type is...

My seat number is...

The distance I am flying is...

Pilot's Comments

....

....

....

....

....

....

....

....

Flight Details

Today's date is...

I am flying from...

I am flying to...

The length of the flight is..

My flight number is..

The airline is...

The aircraft type is...

My seat number is..

The distance I am flying is..

Pilot's Comments

....

....

....

....

....

....

....

....

Flight Details

Today's date is...

I am flying from..

I am flying to...

The length of the flight is.............................

My flight number is.....................................

The airline is..

The aircraft type is.....................................

My seat number is.......................................

The distance I am flying is..........................

Pilot's Comments

....

....

....

....

....

....

....

....

Flight Details

Today's date is...
I am flying from...
I am flying to...
The length of the flight is.................................
My flight number is...
The airline is...
The aircraft type is...
My seat number is...
The distance I am flying is.................................

Pilot's Comments

....
....
....
....
....
....
....
....

Flight Details

Today's date is..
I am flying from..
I am flying to..
The length of the flight is..
My flight number is..
The airline is..
The aircraft type is..
My seat number is..
The distance I am flying is..

Pilot's Comments

....
....
....
....
....
....
....
....

Flight Details

Today's date is...

I am flying from...

I am flying to...

The length of the flight is...

My flight number is...

The airline is...

The aircraft type is...

My seat number is...

The distance I am flying is...

Pilot's Comments

....

....

....

....

....

....

....

....

Made in the USA
Lexington, KY
02 May 2019